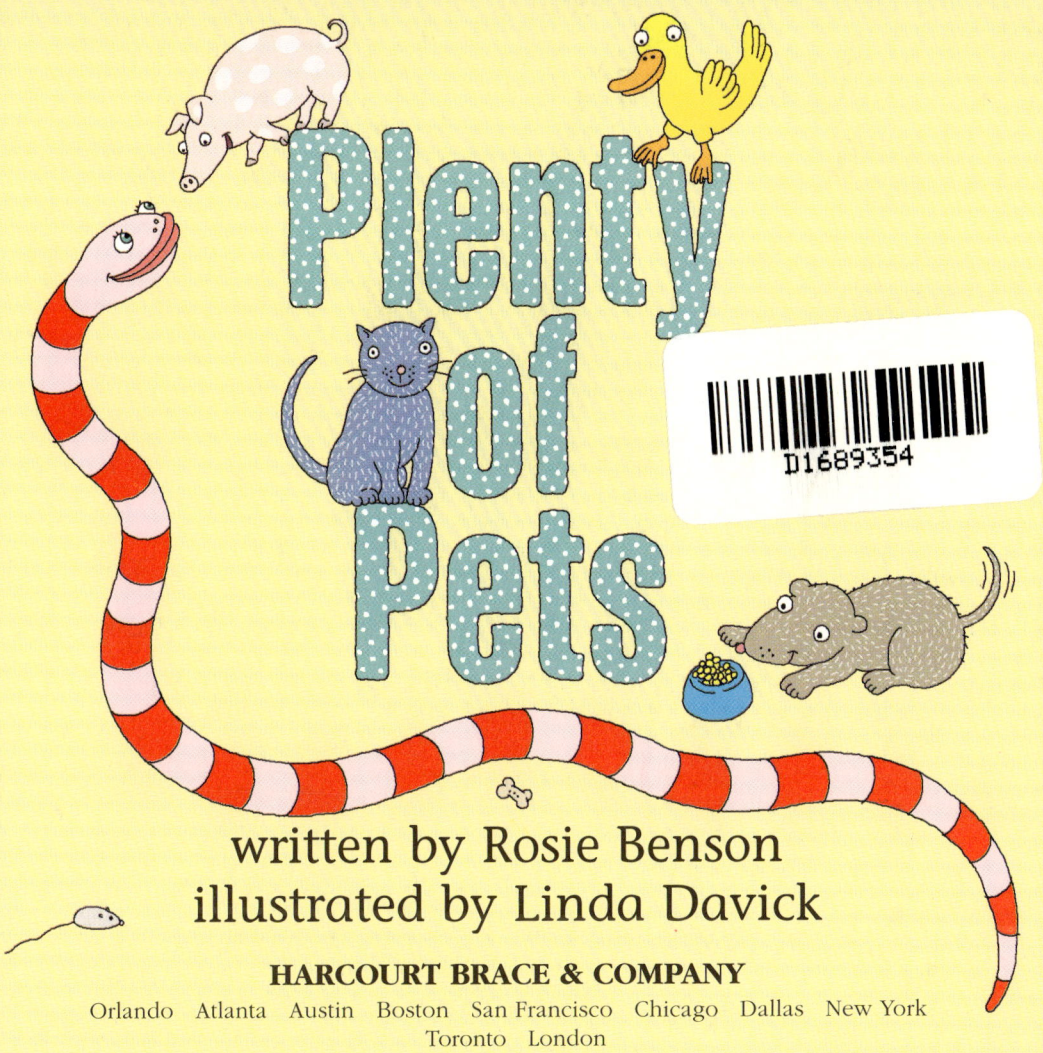

Plenty of Pets

written by Rosie Benson
illustrated by Linda Davick

HARCOURT BRACE & COMPANY

Orlando Atlanta Austin Boston San Francisco Chicago Dallas New York
Toronto London

My mom is a vet.
She helps all kinds of animals.

On Monday Mom came home with a snake.
It needed a new home.

The snake liked to stay on my lap while I read stories to it.

On Tuesday Mom came home with two baby pigs.
They need a new home.

The pigs liked to take a bath, and I scrubbed their little pig ears.

On Wednesday Mom came home with three cats.
They need a new home.

The cats liked to play games, and I watched them get into trouble.

On Thursday Mom came home with four ducks.
They need a new home.

The ducks liked the water, so I took them to the pond to swim.

On Friday Mom came home with five puppies.
They need a new home.

The puppies liked to cuddle, so
I scratched their heads and stomachs.

On Saturday Dad made some telephone calls.
All of the animals need new homes.